DI055548

Crescendos *and* Diminuendos

Crescendos *and* Diminuendos

MEDITATIONS FOR MUSICIANS AND MUSIC LOVERS

Jack Coleman

BakerBooks
Grand Rapids, Michigan

© 2007 by the estate of Jack Coleman

Published by Baker Books
a division of Baker Publishing Group
P.O. Box 6287, Grand Rapids, MI 49516-6287

Printed in the United States of America

All rights reserved. No part of this publication may be reproduced, stored in a retrieval system, or transmitted in any form or by any means—for example, electronic, photocopy, recording—without the prior written permission of the publisher. The only exception is brief quotations in printed reviews.

ISBN: 978-0-7394-9030-3

Unless otherwise indicated, Scripture is taken from the New King James Version. Copyright © 1982 by Thomas Nelson, Inc. Used by permission. All rights reserved.

Scripture marked CEV is taken from the Contemporary English Version © 1991, 1992, 1995 by American Bible Society. Used by permission.

Scripture marked ESV is taken from The Holy Bible, English Standard Version, copyright © 2001 by Crossway Bibles, a division of Good News Publishers. Used by permission. All rights reserved.

Scripture marked KJV is taken from the King James Version of the Bible.

Scripture marked NIV is taken from the HOLY BIBLE, NEW INTERNATIONAL VERSION®. NIV®. Copyright © 1973, 1978, 1984 by International Bible Society. Used by permission of Zondervan. All rights reserved.

Scripture marked TLB is taken from The Living Bible, copyright © 1971. Used by permission of Tyndale House Publishers, Inc., Wheaton, Illinois 60189. All rights reserved.

Interior design by Brian Brunsting

This book is dedicated to my dear wife, Sarah,
whose prayers, suggestions, research, and encouragement
made its completion a reality.

Contents

Contents

Foreword

*B*eginning in my college years and extending through my time with the Billy Graham organization, I have had the God-given opportunity to express my heartfelt love of music. I have used my trombone, sung duets, and led large crusade choirs, and during every session, no matter the size or chosen music, it was essential that I prepare my heart to express joy and direct with integrity and skill, ever mindful that God is the audience. Throughout this long tenure, I have found a musical expression that describes my life: *gioioso*!

It should be no surprise that joy is the essence of the Christian life. God brought to us, through his Son, the gospel of great joy. And Scripture is replete with illustrations of musicians and their role in leading armies or announcing Christ's spectacular birth.

In this book you will find many musical terms, such as *gioioso*, that possess spiritual significance. And this is understandable, because, as Jack Coleman writes, God "is harmony and balance. He is the source of every melodic line and rhythm." John Wesley expressed how central God was to his own compositional work when he wrote the following beside one of his hymns: *Oh let me undivided be, to watch and work and wait for Thee*.

May the same be true of us, in music and in life.

Cliff Barrows

Preface

*H*ow many times have I looked at a musical term on a score and wished that I had some immediate in-depth information on its definition and use? I cannot count the number. It has been frustrating and sometimes embarrassing.

So, I thought I would choose fifty-two of the most used musical terms, one for each week of the year—if that has any special significance—and write about them. It has been very stimulating to see these terms from a new perspective and to realize that each one could be considered in a dimension of spiritual application.

In this application, one factor above all others should remain preeminent in our thinking: the presence of the Lord Jesus Christ. For he is harmony and balance. He is the source of every melodic line and rhythm. He is music in all its depth and multifaceted character.

May the *crescendos* and *diminuendos* of your life experience be controlled by the Lord and may his promised victories be yours.

Jack Coleman

Adagio

(ăh–dah'jŏh)

Literally, "at ease"; at a slow tempo.

$\mathcal{M}$ ost music dictionaries define the tempo of *adagio* in the following way: slower than *andante* (a flowing, walking tempo) and faster than *largo* (very slow). *Adagio* also refers to the second movement of a symphony or a sonata—the *Adagio* movement.

The words "at ease," when used to describe *adagio*, imply not only a tempo but a quality of movement. So, if a musician can think of working the movement of their music between given or established points without stress or tension, then they have attained a quality of "ease." The energies used in a proper musical presentation will be in correct balance and relationship to one another and create a flow of "ease" necessary to a complete *adagio*.

As Christian musicians, we should be in such a right relationship with Jesus Christ that we will be "at ease" with ourselves and our peers. Gone will be the covetous and jealous feelings we might have toward other directors, players, or singers who might have greater success and greater exposure than we.

Our concern will be our love for Jesus Christ and others and the continual improvement of ourselves as his musical servants. Then will come the complete and victorious fulfillment in our lives that he intends for us to have.

> Be kindly affectionate to one another with brotherly love, in honor giving preferences to one another; Not lagging in diligence, fervent in spirit; serving the Lord; rejoicing in hope; patient in tribulation; continuing steadfastly in prayer . . .
>
> Romans 12:10–12

In these days of stress and tension, this kind of affection and brotherly love cannot help but develop a spiritual *adagio*—a quality of ease that should characterize a Christian.

Ad Libitum

An indication giving liberty to the
performer to vary from the strict
tempo. At pleasure. At will.

When a singer or instrumentalist is involved with a passage of a musical composition marked *ad libitum*, they are allowed the freedom to depart from the strict tempos and interpret the music as they see fit. However, any fine musician will take into account the total fabric of the piece and be guided by what they feel the composer intended. They will sing or play from this reference point in a sensitive, tasteful, and artistic way.

As in music, so it is in our Christian walk. The Lord allows us the freedom of choice, but we should keep in mind that these choices must be made with reference to his design for our lives, which is based on the Bible. The harmony of living thus produced will bring a victory in life situations beyond anything one could ask or think.

"What is your music philosophy?" people often ask me. "What kind of 'liberty' may I assume as a Christian musician?"

Second Samuel 24:24 comes to mind:

Neither will I offer burnt offerings to the Lord my God with that which costs me nothing.

My philosophy is that my music must first be worthy of the worship of the Lord. It must edify believers in worship and also be used as a means of evangelism. The technical aspect must be that of excellence so that it might reflect the personality of the Trinity.

And then a warning comes to mind. A warning applicable to when self and not spiritual substance comes into our music. And through Amos, God speaks to us:

I hate your show and pretense—your hypocrisy of honoring me with your religious feasts and solemn assemblies. I will not accept your burnt offerings and thank offerings. I will not look at your offerings of peace. Away with your hymns of praise—they are mere noise to my ears. I will not listen to your music, no matter how lovely it is.

Amos 5:21–23 TLB

The price of liberty is great responsibility to a holy God.

Agitato

(ăh jē tah'tŏh)

Agitated, excited, restless, hurried.

*M*usic bearing a term that implies an agitated, excited, restless, and hurried quality will involve both the performer and the listener through an intensifying of their mental, emotional, and physical responses. This kind of movement in the music will ultimately result in a heightened climax of the tension created, or it will emerge into a calmer resolution.

Life can also become very agitated. Pressures of need and demand and expectation can make living restless and hurried. But, the resolution of this tension will be found through a steadfast faith and trust in Jesus Christ. When the quality of life becomes agitated, it can be surely resolved as we seek the calming presence of the Lord.

Did the apostle Paul resolve the agitation in his life? He writes,

> I have been crucified with Christ; it is no longer I who live, but Christ lives in me.
>
> Galatians 2:20

This simply means that in order to be spiritually effective, one must turn from self and every known sin and live wholly for Christ. Then will the experience of agitation resolve to an inner calm and peace.

If we are to be musical servants whose talents will be used by God for an eternal purpose, only one thing will suffice—that we cast aside our selfish aspirations and glorify God in every musical endeavor.

Alla Breve

(ăhl'lăh brâ'věh)

A tempo mark ₵ indicating quick duple time with the half note rather than the quarter note as the beat.

This term *alla breve* can be confusing if a person ascribes to it a complexity that really isn't inherent in the total picture. One must simply remember that in essence the time signature has become 2/2 instead of 4/4. This means that where there have been four beats to a measure with a quarter note receiving one beat, we now work with two beats in a measure and with the half note receiving one beat.

The crux of the situation is centered on the basic unit of measurement. In the 4/4 measure, the unit of measurement was the quarter note, and in the 2/2 measure, it has become the half note.

Another factor to consider is the time duration of the measure. With a constant tempo being maintained strictly in the performance of the composition involved, the time duration of the basic measure is cut in half when it changes from 4/4 to 2/2.

From the spiritual viewpoint, God's Word can indicate certain changes in our life behavior. Just as *alla breve* functions like a law in music directing us to perform in a certain way, so the application of the Word of God to certain life situations will give us complete directions.

The ignoring of *alla breve* in music can bring about the destruction of the musical structure within which we are functioning. Similarly, the ignoring of the explicit directions of the Word of God can destroy the balanced structure of our lives and make us ineffective cripples.

The key to Christian success is adherence and obedience to him, his Word, and his purposes for life.

Blessed are those who keep His testimonies, who seek Him with the whole heart! You have commanded us to keep Your precepts diligently. Oh, that my ways were directed to keep Your statutes! Your word I have hidden in my heart, that I might not sin against You.

Psalm 119:2, 4, 5, 11

Allargando

(ăhl lar găhn'dŏh)

Slowing down, usually accompanied by a crescendo, used chiefly toward the end of a piece. Growing slower.

The slowing down of a section of music toward the end of a composition, accompanied by an increase in the dynamic level, underscores the finality of a musical thought or concept. Again we must deal with relationships in balance. The retardation of the section involved must be consistent and geared to the increase in the dynamic level. The component parts must mesh.

I have a few musician friends who, because of their age, might be classified as older. They are very young in spirit but chronologically in what we might term latter years.

But, even though life processes might be slowing down somewhat for them, their musical effectiveness becomes stronger. Herein, sometimes, lies the advantage of years. Like the gradual slowing down of an *allargando*, the dynamic level is rising.

I once heard an eighty-year-old man sing a solo in a packed auditorium. The clarity of his voice with its beautiful and steady line, combined with his known love for the Lord, provided an unforgettable experience. His song touched that audience, and the Spirit of the Lord strengthened its impact. A perfect example of *allargando*.

What a blessing to know that

the Lord your God cares . . . from the beginning of the year to the very end of the year.

And this is true year after year. He also grants the promise

as your days, so shall your strength be.

Deuteronomy 11:12; 33:25

Allegro

(ăhl lā grŏh)

Literally, "cheerful." Today employed to indicate quick tempo. Live, brisk, rapid.

*I*t is interesting to note that the *Harvard Dictionary of Music*, in defining *allegro*, states, "Originally a designation for the joyful character of a piece: today employed to indicate quick tempo, regardless of the character and expression. Also used as a title for pieces in quick tempo, especially the first and last movement of a sonata."

In a listing of tempo marks proceeding from the slowest to the quickest, *allegro* is placed in a position faster than *moderato* (moderate) and slower than *presto* (very fast). So, its literal definition of "cheerful" is very correct. That which has a cheerful or joyful character will not be ponderous, heavy, or slow.

Sometimes it is difficult to find a person who is really cheerful these days. Even in Christian circles, the smile and ready handshake or greeting don't happen often enough. Are we so lacking in knowledge of "the joy of the Lord" being our strength, that "he is my strength and my song," that we do not experience the joy from victorious living that results in a cheerful personality?

The Chinese have a proverb. "Man without cheerful face should not open shop!" It is worthy of consideration.

Cheerful also implies *encouragement*. The victorious Christian will be a cheerful person whose desire is to encourage others in the faith. How important it is as Christian musicians to live our lives so people will see our works and glorify our Father in heaven.

What a wonderful God we have—he is the Father of our Lord Jesus Christ, the source of every mercy, and the one who so wonderfully comforts and strengthens us in our hardships and trials. And why does he do this? So that when others are troubled, needing our sympathy and encouragement, we can pass on to them this same help and comfort God has given us.

2 Corinthians 1:3–4 TLB

Andante

Meaning at a walking tempo. A
quarter note with 76 beats per minute.
Moderately slow but flowing.

*D*own through the years there has been some confusion as to the real meaning of *andante*. According to the *Harvard Dictionary of Music*, "there is no agreement among musicians as to whether *andante* belongs to the quick or the slow tempo." One might say it is not positive whether *andante* belongs to the lower side of quick or the upper part of slow.

Dr. Theodore Baker defines *andante* as "going, moving, a tempo mark indicating a moderately slow, easily flowing movement between *adagio* (slow, leisurely) and *allegretto* (moderately fast)." So my conclusion would be *andante*—moderately slow at a walking tempo. And some have suggested, with a metronome marking of m.m. 76.

There should be no confusion that faith in Jesus Christ is often defined as a walk. A walk by faith, if you will. Walking is the means of going from one point to another. It is placing one foot before the other that ultimately constitutes a journey.

In our walk with Jesus Christ, he has delivered his message in a clear, concise manner: "Follow me." By the shores of Galilee he found fishermen busy in their profession. To two of these he said, "Follow me." At Capernaum he said to a busy custom's officer, "Follow me." To a wealthy, influential man who inquired about eternal life and what he must do for it, he directed, "Follow me."

He used those words in his time . . . He uses the same words to you today. One becomes a Christian by following him—never a step farther and never a step less. We walk together. Yet never has he said, "I want to go with you." What he says is, "Follow me." The two words, when obeyed, bring awesome responsibility but great security. And whether the tempo of life is quick or slow, in following him you will have no confusion.

Assai

(ăhs sah'ē)

Very, as "allegro assai"—very fast.

*T*his is a descriptive term that refers to a defined quality of a given situation. Webster states that *very* means "absolute, complete, utter; as, that is the *very* truth."

In music, we are dealing with many variables and factors that must be arranged by the composer, performer, and conductor into a precise system of relationships. Music from the mathematical and acoustical standpoint could be described as a science, for it continually deals with the proper balance of these relationships.

It is the artistic balance of these relationships for which the valid musician is responsible. They must adhere to the concepts of the composer by paying attention to the score and interpreting them with accuracy and excellence. And they should at all times have the "score in his head and not his head in the score."

The term *assai* is almost an absolute. It is saying that quality of tempo or quality of sound should be completely *that* tempo or completely *that* sound. Very . . . allegro *assai*, very fast . . . adagio *assai*, very slow . . . *assai* moderato, very moderate.

In Scripture, we are told that our God is a "very God." When Christ was teaching in the temple, it was asked,

> Do the rulers know indeed that this is the *very* Christ?
>
> John 7:26 KJV, emphasis added

John 14:11 relates,

> Believe me that I am in the Father, and the Father in me: or else believe me for the *very* works' sake.
>
> emphasis added

Our God is "absolute, complete, utterly" with a supply of divine resources to meet all our needs no matter what they might be. *Assai*, or *very*, in this instance means the "ultimate."

A Tempo

(ăh tem'pŏh)

Indicates a return to normal
tempo after deviations within
a section of the piece.

empo, basically, has to do with the rate of speed of a composition or a section thereof, ranging from the slowest to the quickest, as is indicated by tempo marks. Note values are influenced in their time duration by tempo. By the use of the different tempo marks, the duration of any given note value becomes variable within large limits. It is a question of relationships.

The term *a tempo* usually occurs after a deviation from the original or normal tempo of the music composition. It is the responsibility of the musician to have in mind the basic or original tempo and return to th   at after having passed through the change or deviation from the original. The deviation can be faster or slower, but the reference point in *a tempo* is the basic or original tempo.

When a person first accepts Jesus Christ as Savior and Lord, they may experience great joy and peace and a sense of security that stems from the knowledge that God is consistently guiding them as a new Christian in a new life.

The new Christian will grow as they follow the Lord's leading with complete commitment. In so doing, they will find at certain times the Lord moving them more quickly or more slowly than seems normal. But,

> The steps of a good man are ordered by the Lord, and he delights in his way.
>
> Psalm 37:23

However, he will inevitably return us to a normal *tempo* for our lives—a tempo of moderation—a basic tempo. For ours is a God of order and balance and timing.

Attacca

(ăht tăhk'kăh)

Begin the next movement without a break or pause.

*B*alanced movement in music is dependent on an understanding and knowledge of all the factors involved: harmony, rhythm, dynamics, melody, text. The disciplined use of these factors will result in a cohesive tapestry of beautiful sound by which the worship of the Lord can be enhanced.

Sometimes when finishing one section, the word *attacca* will occur, meaning that we do not stop but immediately go on. There is no time for respite but a continuation of concentration and energy in the flow of music. In church choral organizations, the drop-off in attendance after Christmas and Easter is a fact that will break the heart of a choral director. This drop-off is directly related to spiritual motives and spiritual conditions.

We should consider seriously the word *attacca* in our service to the Lord. As Christian musicians—beginning the next movement without a break or pause. But, this demands diligence. Diligence denotes faithfulness. Faithfulness has no room for sporadic commitment. David spoke of diligence.

You have commanded us to keep Your precepts diligently.

Psalm 119:4

Halfhearted effort must be grief to the Savior. The antithesis of diligence is mediocrity. Too many deal with commitment in a mediocre way.

Attacca indicates "keep on." In John 5:17 we read,

Jesus said to them, "My Father is always at his work to this very day, and I, too, am working."

NIV

This allows no room for partial commitment.

Oh, that my ways may be steadfast in keeping your statutes!

Psalm 119:5 ESV

Cantabile

(kăhn tah'bē lĕh)

In a singing style. Lyrical.

When I think of the term *cantabile* I am immediately reminded of the Italian method of vocal pedagogy or teaching called the Bel Canto, or "fine singing." This style is characterized by great breath control, a spinning tone, a forward placement of the vocal line, and a flexibility of the vocal bands that could easily add depth and breadth at any time.

In Italy where the style originated, the training or conditioning of the voice from this Bel Canto style of singing would take five to seven years. But, the end result would remain with the singer for his or her entire life—a conditioned response of the total vocal instrument that by definition is the vocal technique.

Bel Canto was a style that was predominately lyrical but not small dynamically, as some people might assume. It could also be described as beautifully sustained. This is the essence of the term *cantabile*.

As I think of the Christian life I feel that it is *cantabile* by character. It should show a sustaining beauty with great dynamic strength and control, and it should demonstrate a consistent song of praise to the Lord.

O Lord, open my lips, and my mouth shall show forth Your praise.

Psalm 51:15

Coda

(koh'dăh)

A closing passage added to the form
of a composition at the conclusion.
A reinforcement adding finality.

The *coda*, identified as a closing passage added to the form of a composition, can range from a few chords to a long section. It can be simple or complex. Practically all fugues close with a shorter or longer *coda*.

When a composer uses this technique at the close of his music, strength is added to the composition, and there is a reinforcement of the feeling of finality.

In every Christian's life will come the time of great finality when they shall lay down this human body and step into eternity. It is in this transition that the Lord has promised to reinforce, with his love and care, the finality of this life. His strength will be ours, and his peace will make this final section one of great victory.

> Yea, though I walk through the valley of the shadow of death, I will fear no evil; for You are with me . . . Surely goodness and mercy shall follow me all the days of my life; and I will dwell in the house of the Lord forever.
>
> Psalm 23:4, 6

The apostle Paul confidently writes of the coming "spiritual *coda*" for those who believe.

> For to me, to live is Christ, and to die is gain.
>
> Philippians 1:21

Paul's background was pretentious. His writings were prolific. Few individuals in history have prompted so many commentaries, books, and exegeses as Paul, called "the architect of Christianity." However, ending was beginning to him. He desired to be with Christ, which to him was "much better." This is the glorious hope and anticipation of the Christian. We live in the land of the dying and are promoted to the Land of the Living. In stepping across the threshold of eternity, we shall sing praise with the saints and angels for that which God has done for us.

Con Espressione

(kŏhn ĕh spres sē oh'nĕh)

With expression. Sensitivity.

ebster defines *expression* in an interesting way. He says it is the act of pressing or squeezing out, the act or power of representing anything, as by words, sculpture, or music.

How sad it is that we do not take the time to study the music we present to our choirs, or the music that we sing, in a more in-depth way. Preparation becomes a neglected process because we are "too busy" to extract the essence of the lyrics, rhythm, harmonic structure, and melody. We then lack the power to represent music as it was intended.

Without this power based on knowledge and understanding of the music with which we are involved, we lose the quality of expression and sensitivity so necessary for a musical presentation marked by spiritual integrity and excellence.

It becomes a weak facsimile of the original.

Across the top of the front entrance of a building on the campus of USC is a statement: "Art is but a shadow of Divine perfection."

When we work from a position of shallow preparation with the resultant loss of sensitivity, then we become less than a shadow of the kind of excellence the Lord requires of us.

The Bible tells us to

be diligent to present yourself approved to God, a worker who does not need to be ashamed.

Another translation of 2 Timothy 2:15 relates,

Do your best to win God's approval.

CEV

When I first started on an instrument, the words would echo from various places in my house—"practice makes perfect." You can surely relate to similar experiences in your early musical years.

In Christ, we are daily becoming what he has already made us—complete in him. We must practice the presence of God, study to be competent musicians, and as servants express his love to others.

Crescendo

(crěh shen'dŏh)

Increasing the volume or loudness of a tone. A gradual increase in loudness.

It has been said that the "magical quality of a phrase line is its movement." The *crescendo* is based on movement balanced with an increasing intensity and dynamic level. The direction of the melodic line, the progression of the harmonic structure, and the increase of the dynamic level should all be focused and balanced together.

A *crescendo* initiates an action of all the musical components together toward a greater dynamic level. The result will be an exciting and definitive declaration. It creates interest, variety, and strength.

As one follows the Lord Jesus Christ in a walk of obedience and honest commitment, the phrase line of one's life will have movement toward spiritual objectives and goals. Life will become a balance of harmonic progression. Victorious achievement will be gained, and all will be characterized by a strength similar to a mighty *crescendo*.

Let us not forget that it is Jesus Christ who supplies the strength and the power for the victory that he wants each of us to experience.

Martin Luther, writer of so many great hymns, expressed:

> Did we in our own strength confide,
> Our striving would be losing;
> Were not the right Man on our side,
> The Man of God's own choosing.
> Dost ask who that my be?
> Christ Jesus, it is He;
> Lord Sabaoth His name,
> From age to age the same,
> And He must win the battle.

It is in his strength that we operate.

The Lord is the strength of my life . . . The Lord will give strength to His people; the Lord will bless His people with peace.

Psalm 27:1; 29:11

Da Capo

(dah kah'pŏh)

From the beginning. A sign of repetition. Repeating a piece from the beginning to the end (if there is no "fine").

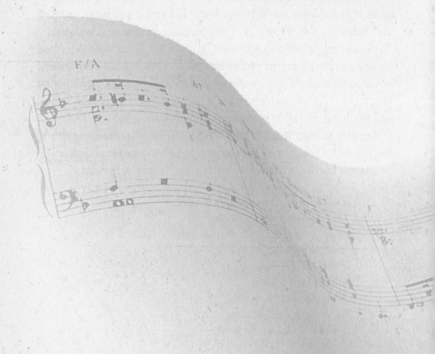

Da capo or *D.C.* indicates a return to the beginning by the performer to reiterate a previous statement. Many times it will give the singer, instrumentalist, or director another chance to traverse a section with renewed determination.

Repetition is a major factor of learning. In the teaching of voice, the repetitious and continuous use of selected scales over a period of time will produce what psychologists define as a "conditioned response." A habit pattern will have been established neurologically and muscularly, and when the singer performs, that "habit pattern" will in essence be his "vocal technique." It is achieved through repetitious exercise.

From the spiritual aspect, the Lord may sometimes train us by placing a *da capo* in our lives indicating a return to the beginning and the repeating of a journey over previously covered ground. In this way one learns, and it is in learning that we grow and progress. It is in that progress that we can meet the standards of excellence commensurate with his name.

Talent, and the level of commitment to its improvement, will bring about certain degrees of technical proficiency. Some will meet standards of excellence. Others will not. Some will have excuses for their mediocrity. Others will rise to heights that did not seem possible. But, through it all, one will find that excellence is based upon work, and that work involves repetition after repetition after repetition.

It is no wonder we are told to "study," to "meditate," to "hear" the Word of God and take it into our hearts. From these repetitions we

[increase] in wisdom and stature, and in favor with God and men.

Luke 2:52

D.C. Al Fine

(D.C. ăhl fē něh)

From the beginning to the place marked "Fine." (End.)

D.C. is an abbreviation for "da capo" meaning the head or the beginning. As a young musician with a smattering of knowledge, I would run into the *D.C. al fine* marking, usually at a repeat bar. Under pressure I would ask myself, "Where do I go now?" The answer is that one returns to the beginning of the piece and plays, sings, or directs it from the beginning to the end—the place marked "fine." It is a repetition, sometimes with additions or extensions, of that which we have just covered.

Life is a framework of time within which we must operate. As a Christian I have grievously sinned. The directions are always the same: return to the beginning, or the One who heads that beginning, and ask his forgiveness. Get up and continue steadfast to the end.

God will provide the grace, compassion, forgiveness, and strength for our walk of faith from the beginning to the end.

Recall the story of Jacob in Genesis 35. At that point in Jacob's life, he was realizing his past of sin and disobedience. God said to him,

Arise, go up to Bethel and dwell there.

Genesis 35:1

In leaving Bethel previously, Jacob had started on a path that met with his own approval rather than God's.

Today, could it be that you are in need of a "*D.C. al fine*"—a new beginning? If your fellowship with a loving Lord has been impaired, why not arise and go to Bethel—wherever it may be for you—the place of loving communion with a waiting Savior?

"For a mere moment I have forsaken you, but with great mercies I will gather you. With a little wrath I hid My face from you for a moment; but with everlasting kindness I will have mercy on you," says the Lord, your Redeemer.

Isaiah 54:7–8

Dal Segno

(dahl sān yŏh)

Repeat beginning at the sign.

*H*ow many times have you been sight-reading a piece of music and come to the term *dal segno* or the letters, *D.S.*? Perhaps, like me, you have turned back through the preceding measures looking desperately for the "sign." Eventually one sheepishly finds it, but the search can be embarrassing. Sometimes the publisher prints the sign too small, causing it to blend visually with the chord symbols. But this should not be used as an excuse!

The problem can be solved in a better way. Examine the music thoroughly before playing or singing it. Look for the signs and the repeats and pattern and form of the composition. Then read it.

God has a definite predetermined pattern for our lives, and he has signs for us to observe. These signs can be found in his Word, our hearts, and often in life situations.

But sometimes life signs are more difficult to discern than music symbols. As the psalmist wrote,

> I am but a pilgrim here on earth: how I need a map.
>
> Psalm 119:19 TLB

What a blessing to know that God has not only provided a guidebook, but more—he has provided guide service. Our map contains God's written instructions. Our Guide, the Holy Spirit, faithfully interprets those instructions for us. Scores of Christians possess the map but ignore the Holy Spirit, who came to indwell the day we took Christ as our Savior. Somehow his signs tend to blend into the busyness of life if we are not sensitive to his presence. Even as true musicianship involves examining music, true discipleship demands the examining of oneself and thus makes it possible for God's plan to overshadow my plan. I must continually look for the signs from the One who

> is at work within you, helping you want to obey him, and then helping you do what he wants.
>
> Philippians 2:13 TLB

D.S. Al Fine

(D.S. ăhl fē něh)

Go back to the sign and continue
to the place marked "Fine."

Occasionally in music we will run into a sign that reads "*D.S. al fine.*" This means that we are to go back to the place where the sign is located and continue from there to the end of the composition.

In our Christian walk there may be times when the Lord will ask us to begin again and with renewed strength continue, by faith, to the end. Some of the tasks are humanly difficult. Relationships can be trying, and often we ask ourselves, Why me, Lord? Why must I work with a choir that lacks commitment? Why go back and start over and over and over again?

At these times I am reminded that "the will of God does not lead us where the grace of God cannot keep us." There was a time in my career when I wanted to escape a certain situation. The battle was heavy and the enemies were real. In my own heart I made the decision to bring this situation to a close. But, I prayed, reluctantly but specifically, "Lord, your will."

In the ensuing days, three specific things transpired that made me confident that I was to "go back to the sign" and continue until he placed a "*fine*" in my path.

As a composer, conductor, and vocal coach, the "whys" sometimes lie heavy upon my heart. It is then I must stop and go back to the cross, the sign of the greatest love and sacrifice. It is at Calvary that all my questions can be resolved and I can continue on toward the end.

> And can it be that I should gain
> an interest in the Savior's blood.
> Died he for me, who caused his pain?
> For me, who Him to death pursued?
> Amazing love! how can it be
> that Thou my God shouldst die for me?
>
> Charles Wesley

In this is love, not that we loved God, but that he loved us and sent His Son.

1 John 4:10

Diminuendo

(dē mē noo en'dŏh)

Becoming gradually quieter.
Interchangeable with decrescendo.

*O*ne of the most difficult vocal techniques for a choir member or soloist to achieve is the ability to sing a *diminuendo* with control and evenness. The vocal mechanism must be trained to do this through consistent daily practice.

Singing a sustained note from a *fortissimo* dynamic level to a *pianissimo*, as one mentally counts or taps his hand in a steady meter, will bring about that conditioned response. The impulse of the counting or tapping will cause *diminuendo* to take place with a consistent diminution. Over a period of time, the voice will be able to produce a beautifully controlled and balanced *diminuendo*.

The schedule of our lives is often frantic because of musical responsibilities: practicing, vocalizing, rehearsing, directing, and making a living. The spiritual quality of life becomes raucous. We therefore must practice moving into times of quiet where the Lord can speak to us, and we to him.

The psalmist wrote,

> Be still, and know that I am God.
>
> Psalm 46:10

We know so little of silence in the busy, noisy, crowded schedule in which we live. We are desperately planning and busily talking when we need to be quietly listening and attentively praying.

Consider that amazing and unique instrument called the brain. It is a sophisticated listening device given to us by God to use. It acts almost like a computer, programming responses, feeding impressions, questioning senses . . . How long has it been since it was in a receptive state?

We are admonished to "study to be quiet." That takes concentration and persistence. It is in this spiritual *diminuendo* that we can assimilate God's power and find great spiritual and musical victories.

Divisi

(dē vē'zē)

Divided. When two parts are written on one stave, to ensure they are not being played as double stops by one instrument, they are marked "divisi."

Divisi is a simple term of instruction to be followed simply. If a composer or arranger has indicated two parts to be played on the first violin staff, and does not want to create technical problems for the players, then they use the term *divisi*. This will place one group of first violins on one note and another group on the remaining note. It will be the responsibility of the conductor to assign the players to each of the notes according to the balance desired.

In a four-part vocal arrangement for men's chorus, the same technique can be used. If the composer or arranger wishes to have the first tenors sing two different notes he can indicate *divisi*, and the conductor can assign the two notes to his singers based on his concept of tonal and vocal balance.

In Webster's definition of the word *divide* in relation to music, he states, "To render with variations and divisions." Most assuredly, the use of *divisi* will bring a variation that will result in greater interest. And sometimes the division of effort can bring greater artistic results.

As we yield our talents to the Lord Jesus Christ, he will not only divide them and multiply them to his use, but he will also empower them with a strength we could never have imagined.

The Word of God could be considered a "Master Score." As the Divine Conductor, he perfects that which concerns us.

> For it is God who works in you both to will and to do for His good pleasure.
>
> Philippians 2:13

Then will he multiply our talents.

> The Lord God of your fathers make you a thousand times more numerous than you are, and bless you as he has promised you!
>
> Deuteronomy 1:11

Dolce

(dŏhl'chĕh)

Sweet and soft. In passages
of quiet tenderness.

*M*usic is an art of contrasts. This is often denied by the contemporary musician involved in the rock idiom, where loud and louder are the only two workable dynamic levels.

In life we find extremes of tension and release. There are often contrasts like fast and slow, high and low, loud and soft, light and dark. These are component parts to the tapestry of life—if you will.

It is in the quiet, tender moments of life when Christ can speak to us the most effectively. When the heart, mind, and body are disengaged from the battle, and subsequently focused toward him, then he can cleanse, forgive, and restore us from our rebelliousness. In these quiet moments we can determine more clearly the ways in which he would have us serve him.

First Samuel 16 carried an interesting vignette about King Saul. He had become desperately troubled by an evil spirit. His servants recommended they seek a man whom they knew was a competent harpist.

> It shall be that he will play it with his hand . . . and you shall be well.
>
> 1 Samuel 16:16

Later we are told that the "sweet, soft" music refreshed Saul, and he was well.

What a contrast—the sound of the harp opposed to the raging evil spirit. Music had its calming effect.

In my years of conducting, listeners have responded more intensely to musical passages of quiet tenderness than to climaxes of great fortissimos. I am sure there is a definite message here!

Fermata

(fâr mah'tăh)

A pause. A prolonging of the measure value of a note or rest, dependent upon the taste of the performer; indicated by a sign placed over ⌒ or under ⌣ the note, rest, or chord.

The pause in music indicated by a *fermata* sign is a very useful tool for musicians in that it offers variation in movement and intensity. It gives respite to a certain character or mood of music established by its rhythm, dynamic level, or harmonic structure. It provides opportunity for new and exciting entrances to subsequent passages.

In our physical and spiritual lives there are times when we must pause and evaluate our relationship with the Lord, our ministry and its effectiveness, our relationship with those surrounding us, and, basically, the way we are proceeding in this life. We must allow God to speak to us in a state of receptiveness and calm. The result will be new energies, new beginnings, and new experiences of fellowship with God the Father through his Son Jesus Christ. Subsequent areas of service will be opened to us with victories assured as we closely follow his direction.

Pause and reflect on these lines . . .

> I counted dollars while God counted crosses;
> I counted gain while he counted losses.
> I counted my worth by the music I'd stored.
> But he sized me up by the scars that I bore.
>
> I coveted crowds and sought for degrees;
> He wept as he counted the hours on my knees.
> I never knew until one day by the grave
> How vain are the things that we spent life to save.

What will it profit a man if he gains the whole world, and loses his own soul?

Mark 8:36

We can make our plans, but the final outcome is in God's hands. We can always "prove" that we are right, but is the Lord convinced? Commit your work to the Lord, then it will succeed.

Proverbs 16:1–3 TLB

Forte Piano

(fôhr'těh–pē ǎn nŏh)

Accent strongly, diminishing immediately to piano. Loud, then suddenly soft.

*I*n this instance, strength with control will bring about the desired result. One can describe *forte piano* as the sudden application of pressure and then release. It is the surprising occurrence of tension followed by immediate relaxation. It is like the blow of a rubber-headed hammer and the resultant bounce-off from the object hit.

We are dealing with techniques and skill in this musical framework, and as directors we should be able to demonstrate vocally for our singers or instrumentally for our players. One can verbalize in an extended and elaborate procedure as to how a *forte piano* should be executed, but the skillful musical demonstration will accomplish the purpose immediately.

I think of the fireworks at Disneyland on a summer evening. Always at the end of the show will be the beautiful starbursts—a sudden explosion of the missile high in the air, the immediate quiet spread of a colorful star-flower expanding in all its beauty. This is *forte piano*.

There will be a coming again in the skies by the Lord Jesus Christ for his church. It will be sudden. Sudden, as revealed in Scripture. The prophets predicted it, Christ promised it, apostles proclaimed it, heaven preached it, and Christians continue to expect it. As he announced his death, so he prophetically told of his return.

Three times, in the last chapter of Revelation, he affirms this.

Surely I am coming quickly.

> Revelation 22:20

It will be a sudden time with the beginning of an immediate release from the tensions and pressures of life. Yes, that will be the final victory, because of Jesus Christ.

Fortissimo

(fohr tis'sē mŏh)

Very loud, usually indicated ff.

I once stood about thirty yards to the left and slightly in front of an Army 105 millimeter Howitzer as it was fired. I shall never forget the all-engulfing impact of this explosion as the shell was propelled five to six miles in the distance.

The pain in my right ear persisted for twenty-four hours, and an annoying buzzing for a couple of days more. Then normal hearing returned.

How loud is very loud? My memory tells me that I have experienced the extreme in loudness. But I also realize it was a controlled extreme. The shell from the Howitzer was aimed at a target.

When we sing or play a *fortissimo* passage, it must be controlled. That control is based on a balance of texture, resonance, timbre, intensity, intonation, and energy—all in relation to the sections that have preceded and that will follow our particular location in the composition. Too many times we lose perspective and balance, and *fortissimo* becomes too loud. Then all the true musical relationships involved are distorted.

"What you are speaks so loudly that I cannot hear what you say" is a familiar quote. The truth of our lives as Christian musicians will ultimately come through loud and clear. It will be evident in every musical performance or presentation.

> Walk worthy of the calling with which you were called, with all lowliness and gentleness, with longsuffering, bearing with one another in love, endeavoring to keep the unity of the Spirit in the bond of peace.
>
> Ephesians 4:1–3

Gioioso

(jŏh yŏh'sŏh)

Joyous, joyfully.

One of the greatest strengths a conductor can have is a basic joy within their heart while preparing and directing their musical organization. For the Christian musician, that joy will stem from a right relationship with Christ, a warm fellowship with the members of the musical group involved, a high standard of performance, and the realization that all are united in a common effort under God's blessing.

Only then will a passage of music marked *gioioso* have validity in regards to the essence of its indicated mood and character. How many times have you feigned joy in directing a choir or in singing when joy was not truly present in your heart? This lack of joy may be very evident to a sensitive, informed listener. When joy is present in a musical performance, a certain chemistry will emerge to bind together all the subtle factors of the composition and its presentation. When it is absent, there is the possibility that threads of tone and harmony will unravel disastrously. Thus, the work of God's Holy Spirit will be stifled and made of little effect in the heart of the listener.

What a responsibility we have to align ourselves in such a way with the Lord that his joy will be the dominating strength of our praise and worship through music.

Gioioso—joyfully, joyously, a term that should describe our lives.

Make a joyful noise unto the Lord . . . Come before his presence with singing.

Psalm 100:1–2

And the ransomed of the Lord shall return, and come to Zion with singing. With everlasting joy . . . they shall obtain joy and gladness, and sorrow and sighing shall flee away.

Isaiah 35:10

Largo

(lar'gŏh)

A slow and broad tempo combined
with great expressiveness.
The slowest tempo mark.

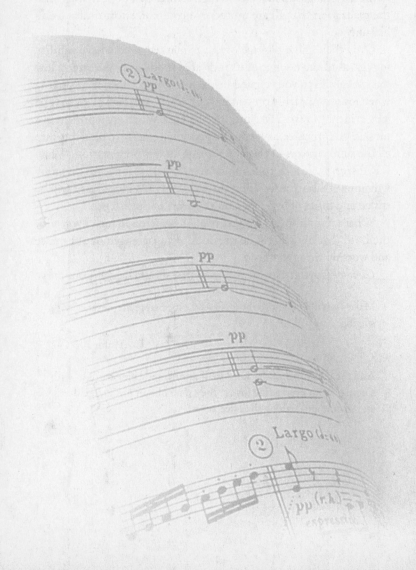

There are usually nine Italian terms to express the entire range of musical tempo. *Largo* is the slowest:

Largo	Broad
Lento	Slow
Adagio	Slow; literally at ease
Andante	Walking
Moderato	Moderate
Allegretto, Allegro	Quick, literally cheerful
Presto	Very fast
Prestissimo	As fast as possible

In addition to these are terms that indicate a gradual change in speed. *Ritardando* means slackening. *Accelerando* means quickening. A deliberate unsteadiness in the tempo is indicated by *rubato*.

A *largo* tempo in a choral organization can reveal vocal problems that will result in poor intonation. Always the poor intonation will be on the flat side. The majority of singers in a church choir think that singing slowly at a *largo* tempo means a relaxing of the expenditure of energies. They "let" down.

Only the opposite approach is valid. Singing *largo* means a more intense application of energy. The singer's posture must be erect with the rib cage lifted; the diaphragm must expand upon inhalation and remain extended as one sustains the tone, the abdominal muscles and sometimes the gluteal muscles must be contracted, the line of the voice must be placed forward and not allowed to emanate from the "back of the throat." These techniques will prevent flat singing and create an exciting *largo* tempo.

A slow pace is a pace of wisdom at times in our lives. Reflecting in the quiet, deep pools of God's restorative love and omniscience is a must for musicians. Harkening—i.e., listening to and obeying his will—is our minimal service, which will make the impact of our music at maximum.

Learn to do good.

Isaiah 1:17

Legato
(lĕh gah'tŏh)

In a smooth, sustained, connected manner without any perceptible interruption between the notes.

The beauty of a phrase line played or sung in a *legato* manner is the identifying mark of a memorable musical performance. Any average musician can present music in a chopped approach with little thought of the shape, contour, or movement of the melodic line.

A musician is a sculptor of sound. The ultimate form of his music will reflect his sensitivity to the beauty of sustained musical passages. It reveals understanding, restraint, and control.

From the spiritual standpoint, a like comparison can be made. A frantic and chopped approach to one's walk in Christ will result in frustration and sometimes defeat. A smooth, sustained walk with the Lord Jesus Christ will bring a joyous momentum that will lead to victorious climaxes and spiritual objectives. The power and energy will be received from the Holy Spirit. The application of the power with knowledge, restraint, and control is dependent on the individual believer.

What a comfort that the Master Arranger can make smooth the rough places of life, like a *legato* passage of music. In so doing, he sustains us with knowledge and power.

Comfort ye, comfort ye my people, saith your God. . . . The voice of him that crieth in the wilderness, Prepare ye the way of the LORD, make straight in the desert a highway for our God. Every valley shall be exalted, and every mountain and hill shall be made low; and the crooked shall be made straight, and the rough places plain: And the glory of the LORD shall be revealed, and all flesh shall see it together; for the mouth of the LORD hath spoken it.

Isaiah 40:1, 3–5 KJV

Leggiero

(led jâh'drŏh)

Lightly. Airy. Graceful with a slight pressure of the key or of the bow, with a touch of non legato.

Many times I have watched the hummingbirds in our garden move from flower to flower with a delicate lightness. With wings vibrating at a very rapid rate they will remain at one fixed altitude or distance from a rose. They will take from the flower the nectar desired and then lightly fly to another location. This most certainly describes the essence of *leggiero*.

In our definition we read "and with a touch of non legato." This does not mean that a phrase sung or played should be represented by notes that are detached. It simply tells us that the cohesive line of regular legato is less heavy when sung or played *leggiero*. It infers delicacy as well as gracefulness.

There is a delicacy in the great compassionate love of Jesus Christ. It is binding and yet without a heaviness.

Years ago, a contemporary song that was listed in the top forty had the lyrics, "He ain't heavy, he's my brother." And so, the love of Christ has that lightness with unparalleled strength.

> Oh the deep, deep love of Jesus—
> Vast, unmeasured, boundless, free!
> Rolling as a mighty ocean
> In its fullness over me.
> Underneath me, all around me
> Is the current of Thy love—
> Leading onward, leading homeward
> To my glorious rest above.
>
> S. Trevor Francis

God *is* love!

And we have known and believed the love that God has for us. God is love, and he who abides in love abides in God, and God in him. Love has been perfected among us in this.

1 John 4:16–17

Lento

(len'tŏh)

Slow. Often peaceful and reflective.

*M*usic is an art form through which many contrasting emotional moods can be expressed. Tempos are the catalysts whereby these moods can be developed.

Very rapid tempos will denote moods of great intensity. Moderate or slower speeds can imply a deliberateness of action—in the case of *lento* (slow), a reflection.

However, if a *lento* or slow tempo is used, a musician must not allow the fabric or structure of the music to disintegrate. His approach must supply a cohesiveness that will hold the music together.

The tempo of the life of a musician is usually very intense. There is a speed and an excitement in preparation for performance that many times will rob us of the benefits of a deliberate or slower approach.

Because of the intense nature of the business, many arrangers that I have been associated with in Hollywood, Christian and non-Christian alike, work on their projects straight through the day and night before a recording session. This happens for a variety of reasons: last-minute changes for a client, the availability of players, etc. They then walk into the studio with the ink still wet on the instrumental parts from the music copyist's pen. And a few take pride in the fact that they have not slept for twenty-four hours because of the frantic preparation.

Our Lord intends for us to work slowly and completely at times—most assuredly on schedule—not always at a robbing and debilitating pace. The places of slow deliberateness afford us the opportunity of the clarity of his voice. The resultant cohesiveness will afford us great musical and spiritual victories.

Be still and know that I am God.

Psalm 46:10

God has called us to peace.

1 Corinthians 7:15

Maestoso

(măh ĕ stoh'sōh)

Majestic, dignified. In a style
characterized by lofty breadth.

We were aboard a liberty ship just off the coast of Normandy, France, one dark night during World War II when a German plane flew over the area and dropped five bombs. I was asleep in the rear hold of the ship when the first bomb exploded to our right. The second was a little closer, and the third at our side. The sound of the explosions was like the making of a catastrophe of the human mind.

The fourth bomb missed us as it landed to the left of the ship, and the fifth exploded a little farther on. The ensuing silence was like a dark paralysis.

It was between the explosion of the third bomb to the right and the fourth bomb on the left that it appeared to me that the very curtain of eternity had been parted, and I found myself in the immediate presence of the awesome majesty of a holy God. His hand seemed extended, and it was as if he was holding my heart in that holy hand.

My approach to music has forever been influenced by that experience. When we conduct, sing, or play music representative of God the Father and the Lord Jesus Christ, the majesty of a just and loving God should pervade it.

Whenever we are involved with the musical term *maestoso*, his majesty and greatness should be paramount in the texture of the sound we produce.

In daily living, our character and personality must reveal the evidences of his majestic presence in our hearts.

Now to Him who is able to keep you from stumbling, and to present you faultless before the presence of His glory with exceeding joy, to God our Savior, who alone is wise, be glory and majesty, dominion and power, both now and forever.

Jude 24–25

Marcato

(mar kăh'tŏh)

Marked, emphasized; separating
and emphasizing each note.

*H*ow many times have I conducted a piece of music with the thought it must be completely cohesive with a strong legato concept? I remember preparing a small vocal ensemble for a recording session at RCA studios in Hollywood with this approach.

As soon as the group was asked to do a sound check over the mikes, the producer made us aware that the blend was so sustained that some of the words could not be understood. "Hit the words a little harder—emphasize them," he said. The problem was corrected. We sang a little more *marcato*.

A marked emphasis must be applied to areas of our Christian life that will have a revolutionary effect in our total spiritual growth. The quiet reading of God's Word, the trusting time of conversation with the Lord, the stepping away from the egocentricity of the life of an effective musician—these will result in greater effectiveness where it counts—for eternity.

We need to emphasize that unless the Spirit of the Lord touches our works, they are in vain.

> "Not by might nor by power, but by My Spirit," says the Lord of hosts.
>
> Zechariah 4:6

> Call to me, and I will answer you, and show you great and mighty things, which you do not know.
>
> Jeremiah 33:3

Meno

(mā'nǒh)

Less, as "meno mosso." Less quickly.

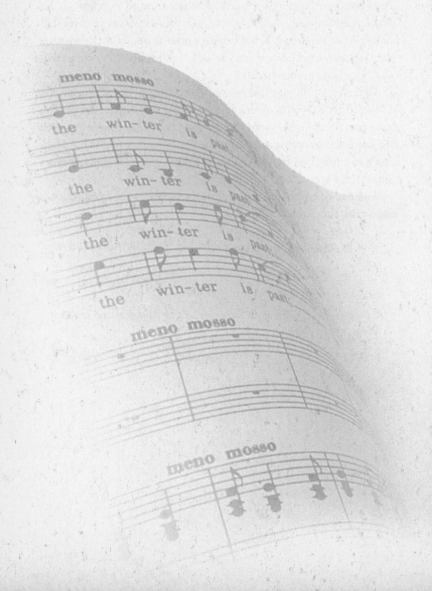

I have heard musicians discussing other performers or musical organizations and saying, "The only thing they can do is sing loud or louder. The only thing they do well is play fortissimo. There is little contrast."

Music is an art of contrasts, and particularly in the area of dynamics and tempos. We are inclined to approach a composition with the right motivation concerning all of its component parts, but sometimes the end result is a sameness in texture, tempo, and dynamics. Restraint as indicated by the term *meno* is missing, and this leaves us with an uninteresting block of musical sound, like a painting without colors of different shades and hues.

Restraint infers less with the presence of great control. Less of us is sometimes required by the Lord Jesus Christ. We have a tendency to project our personal plans and wishes into our lives, but he asks us to walk with less of ourselves and all of himself. Restraint as regards our egos in the music we conduct or perform will allow the Lord to use us in a way far beyond anything we could expect or envision. Less of oneself and all of Christ will ensure this, and we will discover his control as the greatest blessing of all.

An old hymn writer expressed it like this:

Oh the bitter pain and sorrow that a time could ever be
When I proudly said to Jesus, "All of self, and none of Thee."

Yet He found me; I beheld Him, bleeding on the accursed tree,
And my wistful heart said faintly, "Some of self, and some of Thee."

Day by day His tender mercy, healing, helping, full and free,
Brought me lower, while I whispered, "Less of self and more of Thee."

Higher than the highest heavens, deeper than the deepest sea,
Lord, Thy love at last has conquered: "None of self, and all of Thee."

James McGranahan

Moderato

(mŏh dĕh rah tŏh)

In moderate speed, between andante (a walking tempo) and allegro (a quick tempo).

*F*or many church musicians, indicated tempos often have vague meanings. We often work within the parameters of our own feelings, biases, and limited understandings of the total piece of music—and if the composer were to hear it, he would be shocked at the difference from his original concept of the composition. He might also feel that the director had an unwarranted gall in doing it that way.

There must be a careful moderation with all tempos. By that I mean a musician should be aware of metronome markings of indicated tempos and adhere to the wishes of the composer. If it is *moderato* you are working with, then be sure that the music is directed between *andante* and *allegro*.

An adherence to the laws of God as indicated in his Word cannot be cast aside as having vague meanings in the direction of our lives. Nor do we have the license to interpret his Word from our bias or emotional feelings. His Word is final revelation and must be heeded and acknowledged through our daily lives.

> I delight to do Your will, O my God; and Your law is within my heart. I have declared Your faithfulness and Your salvation; I have not concealed Your lovingkindness and Your truth from the great congregation. Do not withhold Your tender mercies from me, O Lord: let Your lovingkindness and Your truth continually preserve me.
>
> Psalm 40:8, 10–11

Mosso

(môhs'sŏh)

Movement (in relation to
speed). Molto mosso—very fast.
Meno mosso—less fast.

I have looked at this term many times, and it never comes across to me as having to do with speed. Yet the essence of its definition means speed and movement.

Movement is related to the rate of speed or momentum most suitable for a given composition. *Mosso* tells us that we should move rapidly within the framework of the composition.

In landing a plane, the pilot must maintain a definitive speed in order to touch down without a problem. Sometimes he must increase the speed of the plane (molto) to keep from stalling and spinning into the ground. At other times he must slow the speed of the plane (meno) to keep from floating as he attempts to set it down. At all times he is dealing with a basic speed that will allow him to bring the ship in safely.

Once a person has accepted Jesus Christ as Lord, a movement has begun within a framework of eternal life. The speed or tempo is basic and ordered by God the Father. We must adjust to his directions in a movement of love, sacrifice, and service.

We are surrounded by fellow friends and musicians who know nothing of the love of Christ. I wonder what our movement and speed is toward reaching them with the unsearchable message of redemption. It has been said that "God hasn't retained many of us as lawyers, but he has subpoenaed all of us as witnesses for him."

It is a command of the Lord to share his message. This can be done through our music but also through our lives.

Let the redeemed of the Lord say so, whom He has redeemed from the hand of the enemy.

Psalm 107:2

And he commends us for sharing.

Those who are wise shall shine like the brightness of the firmament, and those who turn many to righteousness like the stars forever and ever.

Daniel 12:3

Molto

(mŏhl'tŏh)

Much, very intensely. "Molto allegro"—very quickly.

*I*n order to achieve the proper effect indicated by the term *molto*, the rest of a composition must be understood in its component parts of tempo, rhythm, intensity, dynamics, and mood.

Balance is the prime factor involved, and this demands a complete knowledge of the total fabric of a piece by the singer, instrumentalist, or director.

How big is *molto* (much) in relation to *poco* (little) in the total composition? Understanding the complete concept of the composer will bring about the proper interpretation of all the musical components.

Much is expected of us by our heavenly Father.

> For everyone to whom much is given, from him much will be required.
>
> Luke 12:48

When Jesus Christ is Lord of our lives, the totality of our existence should be in his hands. And a songwriter has indicated that "little is much when God is in it."

With God's leading and our response, we will be directed in a life balanced by his holy will and sustaining strength. Our understanding will be enlightened by our continued walk with him, and the impact of our lives and ministry will then have validity and balance.

> The eyes of your understanding being enlightened; that you may know what is the hope of His calling, what are the riches of the glory of His inheritance in the saints, and what is the exceeding greatness of his power to us who believe, according to the working of His mighty power.
>
> Ephesians 1:18–19

Obbligato

(ŏhb blē gah'tŏh)

A counter melody that complements
the main theme—an accompanying
part, though beautiful, is of secondary
importance to the melody.

The addition of an *obbligato* played by strings, french horns, or woodwinds, in my opinion, certainly enhances any beautiful melody. The melody, if correctly written with musical balance, will have an inherent strength of its own. But the spectrum of its influence can most always be enhanced by a supporting melody usually known as an *obbligato*.

The main factor to be considered with the *obbligato* is that it functions in a position of secondary importance. From the choral or instrumental standpoint, the dynamic level of the *obbligato* must always be slightly less than the main melody. Only then does it have its fullest impact in the balanced fabric of the composition with which we are dealing.

Recently a question was put to me: "How would you react if, within the framework of God's will, you were replaced as the director of your church choir?" In examining my heart, I knew that I would be tremendously bothered by a situation like this. I felt that it would be an ultimate test for a Christian musician. Our egos are so enwrapped in what we do musically.

But, if I am really motivated to serve the Lord, regardless of the position or recognition, then I could easily step down into a supportive role. Like the *obbligato*, my life function should be aimed at only one objective—to serve the Lord Jesus Christ in any way and to *supportively* enhance his message of love and salvation.

May our prayers be like Jabez of old:

And Jabez called on the God of Israel saying, "Oh, that You would bless me indeed, and enlarge my territory, that Your hand would be with me, and that You would keep me from evil, that I may not cause pain!" So God granted him what he requested.

1 Chronicles 4:10

Pianissimo

(pē ah is'se mŏh)

Very softly, usually indicated by PP.

One of the softest, most beautiful sounds in all the world is that of a high performance sailplane passing overhead as a person observes it from the ground. I have flown these marvelously designed ships many times, and the gentleness of the wind past the canopy as heard from inside the cockpit is even more impressive, particularly to a musician.

A sailplane gliding through the atmosphere will produce certain pitches at different speeds. There will be an intense, higher pitch at one hundred miles per hour as contrasted to the soft, caressing sound of the wind at thirty-seven miles per hour—just above stalling for those of you who fly.

Flying at 10,250 feet at a very slow speed late one April afternoon is an experience I shall never forget. As I sat in the small cockpit of that high-performance ship, the brilliantly blue, high vaulted heavens contrasted starkly with the darkening afternoon shadows so far below. The whisper of the wind at that slow speed was like the still small voice of God heard from heaven itself. Truly, it was a soft *pianissimo* with all its beautiful textures.

In our music, *pianissimos* must be like this—controlled yet ever present with an eternal dynamic. And our busy lives in music must slow down at consistent times so the Lord can softly speak to us and we with him. Then we will find new areas to worship and praise him.

Piu

(pew)

More. Example: "Piu lento"
(meaning slower).

The more we become involved in music, the more it demands of us. We shall have to arrange for more practice time, more money for better instruments or teachers, more involvement with other musicians and musical organizations. It is like feeding an insatiable hunger. But, if we are committed, we will grow in the development of our musical skills and techniques. It is an endless quest for "more" of all that music has to offer.

The term *piu* simply means "more." *Piu* can be coupled with allegro, and it will mean "faster" or "quicker." It is a small term by virtue of its composition—three letters—but, it is directive and demanding.

Acknowledging Christ as our Lord and Savior involves more—much more. The new vistas of life and opportunity, the excitement and joy of realizing that God wants to use us, the acceptance of his blessings, the giving to others, the fellowship with believers, is just the beginning. It is the "more" that he has for us.

The greatest "more" will be that of an eternity with a holy God. This will be a time and place in which bad intonation and dissonances will not exist. All will be in harmonic balance, and we will realize that his call to us as musicians was more than a privilege.

> More about Jesus would I know, more of his grace to others show,
> More of his saving fullness see, more of his love who died for me.
>
> More about Jesus let me learn, more of his holy will discern;
> Spirit of God, my teacher be, showing the things of Christ to me.
>
> More about Jesus in his word holding communion with my Lord,
> Hearing his voice in every line, making each faithful saying mine.
>
> Eliza Hewitt

Poco a Poco

(pô'kŏh ah pô'kŏh)

Little by little; by degrees, gradually.

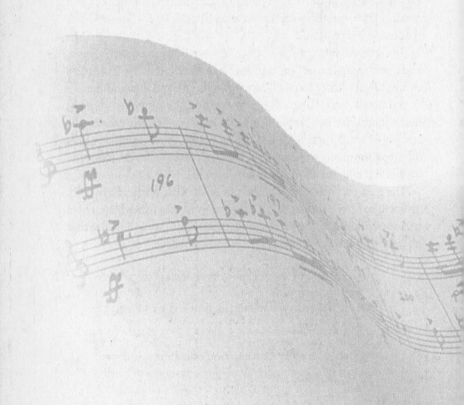

*H*ow little is little? Immediately one must have a reference point and move from there. The situation emerges into one of relationships.

A pilot goes through an established procedure before taking off in his plane. He checks the engine and its magnetos and all the instruments. Then he throttles back and awaits the word from the control tower that will allow him to taxi to the end of the runway and begin another memorable flight.

As he pushes forward on the throttle, the plane begins to move forward. The speed increases little by little until the plane becomes airborne and flight is a reality.

In music when we are asked to increase a tempo or dynamic level *poco a poco*, it means that we are operating in the field of relationships. We must ask ourselves from whence we started and to what objective we are headed. All increases in this kind of situation call for a consistency in the development thereof. We must adhere faithfully to the direction, "little by little."

A walk of faith will result in greater spiritual strength and growth when a person applies themselves "little by little," or as the Scripture states, "line upon line, precept upon precept," with consistency. Securing the "ground we have taken" by a consistent application of persistence in our journey with Christ will allow us to have a more powerful impact and influence in our day.

As you have therefore received Christ Jesus the Lord, so walk in Him.

Colossians 2:6

Rallentando
(răhl len tăhn'dŏh)

Gradually slackening in speed.
With gradually reduced speed.

One of the thrills of flying a high-performance sailplane is the landing. The Polish Jantar 2A is one of the most beautiful ships in all the world, with an enormous wingspan of sixty-seven feet and a single place cockpit. Flying this into the landing pattern of a glider port properly takes skill and planning.

Approaching the touchdown at sixty knots speed, the pilot must be very sensitive on the controls; a slight back pressure on the stick at the flare-out and then the single wheel in the forward middle of the fuselage caresses the earth.

Immediately comes the roll-out with its gradual slackening in speed. Here, one experiences the joy and gratefulness of realizing that another successful flight has been made.

In a section of music where *rallentando* is indicated, the conductor must be sensitive to the tempo or speed they are using just prior to the *rallentando* and plan accordingly. The slackening of speed must be one of relationship and degree. It cannot be done suddenly or without artistic finesse. If the *rallentando* is not handled carefully, the result can be musical awkwardness and embarrassment.

Occasionally, a gradual slackening in the intensity and speed of our lives is a must. The constant outpouring of energies by the musician in the Lord's service, without a break, can have a desperate effect. There is nothing unspiritual about taking times for rest and recuperation. Times of refilling with his energy and the power of his Spirit renew and refresh.

Often Sunday is the busiest day of a musician's week. Therefore, another time must be set aside to let the body regain its expended strength.

Rallentando reminds us to gradually reduce our high involvement and speed.

> Do you not know that your body is the temple of the Holy Spirit who is in you, whom you have from God, and you are not your own? For you were bought at a price; therefore glorify God in your body and in your spirit, which are God's.

> 1 Corinthians 6:19–20

Rubato

(roo–băh'tŏh)

"Robbing" or taking from the notes their strict time value by alternately hurrying, then retarding, for the purpose of expression. It should not depart so far from the tempo as to destroy the sense of rhythm.

In order to re-create a melody or phrase line of a piece of music, an artist may employ the technique of *rubato*. This technique can be used only in places where the music remains uncomplicated in structure. Surely, it cannot be used effectively in a series of runs made up of sixteenth or thirty-second notes.

Rubato as a technique involves moving in and out, ahead and behind the basic structure of tempo and rhythm. The tempo is a guideline that must be followed with consistency. If not, the indicated rhythms will be impaired.

Using *rubato* to re-create a fresh new approach to a section of music that lends itself to this technique is left to the discretion of the artist. Their particular interpretation will have uniqueness because it will be theirs alone. In most instances it will be unlike that of any other performer. Because of this, a musician's *rubato* could identify their style. But it must be done with integrity and taste.

Some pop singers employ *rubato* very effectively. Three examples of this would be Frank Sinatra, Tony Bennett, and Barbra Streisand. All three exhibit great artistry and taste in the use of this technique.

As Christian artists and musicians we must follow the structure of God's Word and use it as a strict guideline. In this attitude of obedience our individual and personal gifts will be used by the Lord in ways that are tremendously unique. The ways in which he will personally use us will be different from the ways in which he will use another person. Nevertheless, he will use us all as Christian musicians, if we walk in obedience to his holy will for our lives. He may move us ahead or keep us behind in his structure of scheduling, but he will instruct us and guide us and cause us to be profitable servants.

I will instruct you and teach you in the way you should go; I will guide you with My eye.

Psalm 32:8

Segue
(sāy-gway)

Proceed to the following movement
without a break; no pause.

I remember hearing the term *segue* for the first time when I was a young singer and musician. I was in a rehearsal for a recording session with a small vocal ensemble when the director said, "We'll omit pages 45 through 48 and *segue* from the bottom of 44 to the top of 49." I had to turn and ask the tenor on my right, who was more experienced than I, just what this word meant.

His answer was, "You go immediately from the one page to the top of the other without stopping. We skip the pages in between."

And so, in a practical situation I had learned something that I should have picked up as a student. Needless to say, I rolled that word around a little in subsequent situations, taking pride in a newly found knowledge.

Life sometimes brings situations in which we have to *segue* without pause. Disappointment, loss, rejection—these are words characterizing events that can bring one to a complete and shocking emotional halt. But, the individual who walks with the Lord Jesus Christ will be given the strength to move on without pause to the next exciting chapter, in spite of pain and human frustration.

Most musicians, by nature, seem to be very sensitive individuals. We appear to experience events and situations on a more intense level of awareness than most others. However, as God's servants we have at our disposal his resources to move indefatigably through every segment of life without pause.

> Fear not; for I have redeemed you; I have called you by your name; you are Mine. When you pass through the waters, I will be with you; and through the rivers, they shall not overflow you. When you walk through the fire, you shall not be burned, nor shall the flame scorch you. For I am the Lord your God.
>
> Isaiah 43:1–3

Semplice

(sem'plē chěh)

In a simple, unaffected manner.

There are times when we as directors of music try to make more of a composition than is indicated by the composer. Instead of keeping it simple, uninvolved, and without ornamentation, we project our concepts into it by increasing or slowing the tempo, changing the dynamic level—or even adjusting the accompaniment.

A young and gifted singer once came to audition for me. He had just returned from singing a supporting role in *Porgy and Bess* with the Houston Opera. He had gained much experience in this role as the group toured Europe for three months.

We met in the choir room of the church where I was conducting, and I asked him if he wanted me to accompany him. He said, "No! I will sing without accompaniment." This immediately aroused an element of surprise in my heart.

He bowed his head and remained quiet for a few moments and then began to sing. In great simplicity, and yet in great emotional and spiritual strength, the beauty of this voice and commitment to the Lord Jesus Christ came pouring forth.

It was as if the room were filled with a complete symphony orchestra in majestic accompaniment. And when he finished, it took some time for an imagined audience to cease their very intense applause. The key? *Simplicity!*

Webster describes the word *simple* as "innocent, guileless, unsophisticated, straightforward, uninvolved, intelligible."

And I realized—these are some of the characteristics of Jesus. They also should be well-defined facets of our lives as Christian musicians.

He must increase, but I must decrease.

John 3:30

Sempre

(sem'prěh)

Always, continually, throughout.

*T*his is one of the least complex of all the musical terms that we musicians must deal with. *Sempre* infers consistency—a quality of completeness.

Sempre can be used with other musical terms. Example: *sempre legato* (always sustained or continually sustained).

However, there is a danger that we might "routinely" allow a boring "sameness" to creep into a section marked *sempre legato*. The vitality and energy used to produce the music should never be allowed to diminish or dissipate into such a condition. Again, the musician must skillfully control this.

The very character of our God can be described by the word *faithful*. He is "always, continually, throughout" faithful to us in his consistent love and concern. He will always sustain us.

Cast your burden on the Lord, and He shall sustain you.

Psalm 55:22

He will continually guide us and protect us.

For He shall give His angels charge over you, to keep you in all your ways.

Psalm 91:11

He will throughout eternity reveal to us his majesty.

Could a musical term define an attribute of God? *Sempre*. He always has been and always will be.

For this is God, our God forever and ever.

Psalm 48:14

Sforzando

(sfŏhr tsăhn'tŏh)

With a sudden and strong accent
on a single note or chord.

The major factors involved with the *sforzando* will be suddenness and strength. This musical term can affirm a definitive musical declaration. It can be compared to a person in conversation underlining a thought by banging his hand down upon a table and saying, "This is the way it is!" It is done with explosive suddenness and strength. *Sforzando* can bring about a completely new and different mood in a musical composition.

In the realm of the spiritual, there are times when the Lord may move in on our lives instantaneously and with great strength. It may be in the form of chastisement or it may be in a miraculous deliverance from danger or situations that would seem humanly impossible to resolve. But when this transpires, a new mood and perspective will be established, and the value of sudden strength used in divine wisdom will become apparent.

In Jeremiah 49:8 we have record of God speaking in suddenness and strength. The enemy was pursuing the Edomites, and panic was in their hearts. God spoke to them: "Dwell deep." These were words of strength suddenly spoken.

As musicians we can mistakenly feel that service is of the greatest importance and become so busy that the really important thing to God, our devotion and fellowship with him, is neglected. In that excessive service we can be overcome with fatigue, and then the enemy will pursue us.

Prayerful preparation of all musical projects will restore energies and result in presentations that are worthy of our Lord. To strive to "dwell deep" in him will give us an explosive, controlled power so necessary in the ministry of music.

Sostenuto

(sŏh stĕh noo'tŏh)

Sustained, prolonged.
Sustaining the tone.

Sustaining a tone or prolonging its character or duration implies a concentrated effort with a controlled expenditure of energy. For the singer this means an alert mind; a committed heart; erect posture with rib cage in a position of elevation, the diaphragm in proper use, the mask of the face slightly lifted, the lower jaw relaxed; and a knowledge of from whence the musical passage has emerged and to where it is going.

This is not achieved by most singers easily. Nor is it perfected without cumulative rehearsal in a choral organization. Not only is the development of the vocal musculature involved but the internal muscular structure of the body must be conditioned as well. The body is the musical instrument and it must be fit to act as one. And this means conditioning through conscious effort and practice. Then sustained tones will be produced in a correct way.

Energy and vitality are involved. The source for both is the human heart. We are told that a "merry heart doeth good like a medicine." This becomes a fact of life for those who really know Christ and who walk in joyful obedience to his will. If there is joy in the heart, then there will usually be energy and vitality in the body.

The presence of God's Holy Spirit in life will be the sustaining source of spiritual strength and energy. This is so important to us as musicians. Seventy-five percent of singing is energy and vitality. As Christians we have ready access to that energy and vitality through prayer. This will sustain us when we are called upon to sustain—whether it be in music or a life situation.

> Spirit of God, descend upon my heart: Wean it from earth, through all its pulses move. Stoop to my weakness, mighty as thou art, And make me love thee as I ought to love.
>
> George Croly

Sotto Voce

(sŏht'tŏh voh'chĕh)

Literally, "under the voice." In performance, a quiet, subdued tone.

*T*his term means vocal or instrumental performance "in an undertone," that is, with subdued sound. We will be involved here with a reduction in the dynamic level. The question is, "How much reduction?"

A strict reference must be made to the dynamic level of the section just prior to the term *sotto voce* and to the section that follows it. Paying attention to the balance of dynamic levels in the execution of the *sotto voce* is the crux.

If we have been employing forte (loud), then *sotto voce* implies that we reduce the degree of loudness to the mid parameters of piano (soft). It must be a function that involves artistic taste and control, and we are the only ones who can "make it happen."

It is reasonable and logical that as Christians we should be skillful in spiritual things. By that, I mean we must have a sensitivity and discernment to the voice of the Lord as he speaks softly to us. Some describe it as "that still small voice." This means quietly listening to him. From that must come the pragmatic application of his counsel and direction to the issues of life. Therein lies the skill. It all might be described as listening with action.

The quiet, subdued witness of the Lord within the heart, plus our ready obedience to do his complete bidding, will result in great spiritual victories.

> I have made you hear new things from this time,
>   Even hidden things, and you did not know them.
>
>   Isaiah 48:6

> Eye has not seen, nor ear heard,
>   Nor have entered into the heart of man
>   The things which God has prepared for those who love
>   Him.
>
>   1 Corinthians 2:9

Subito

(soo bē tŏh)

Suddenly, immediately, unexpectedly.
Like "subito piano"—suddenly soft.

*I*n my career as a musician I have discovered the use of the word *subito* coupled with the word *piano* more often than any other way. Suddenly soft or immediately soft seems to be a tool used by composers to create great contrasts in the dynamic range of a particular composition. This sudden change in dynamics will cause the listener to concentrate more intensely on the performer and his music.

If a public speaker drives home a point with great authority in a very loud voice and then suddenly drops to a whisper in amplifying that point, the emotional and intellectual response on the part of the audience will be very evident by the quietness in the auditorium.

If a singer moves into the climax of a song on a *fortissimo* level, only to suddenly hold the upper note of that final passage on a *pianissimo*, the intensity of concentration by the audience can be almost physically felt.

On the Sea of Galilee Jesus spoke to the elements of the storm, and they immediately became quiet. The disciples who were with him were utterly amazed, and their hearts' attention was intensified by a holy wonder.

When Jesus speaks to us, we should be suddenly and immediately responsive to his leading. Therein lies joy, confidence, and fulfillment; joy in knowing that he wants to use us, confidence toward him, ourselves, and our fellow man.

Speak, Lord, for Your servant hears.

1 Samuel 3:9

Tacet

(tah'cet)

Be silent—do not play. For instruments that are not needed in a movement or long section.

I was in a rehearsal with a very fine orchestra in Southern California one Saturday morning. Everyone was working hard in preparation for a performance the next day. Most of the members of this group were instrumentalists who played regularly in the Hollywood studios.

I came to a section marked *tacet* for the violas and cellos. So, I stopped and turned to these string players and said, "From bar 36 to the end of the section, violas and cellos drop out."

At that point, one of the viola players said, with an edge to his voice, "Violas are *tacet*, Jack?"

Getting his point I answered, "That's right! *Tacet*!"

He was making sure that I used the correct term and thus got my attention, and I came away with the memory of that situation.

So, if we are to be fine conductors, then we must be accurate in giving instructions and leading people who are superior musicians. If we are not fully prepared and are without a complete knowledge of the score, then we lose credibility as Christian musicians. This can tarnish a testimony for Christ.

There will be times in our lives when the Lord may say to us, "*Tacet*" or "Be silent." If one is silent, then they must listen and observe. It is then that we again learn and grow.

Aspire to lead a quiet life.

1 Thessalonians 4:11

The incorruptible beauty of a gentle and quiet spirit, which is very precious in the sight of God.

1 Peter 3:4

In quietness and confidence shall be your strength.

Isaiah 30:15

Troppo

(trŏp'pŏh)

Too much; as "adagio non troppo."
Slow, but not too slow.

I think that the place at which we, as Christian choral directors, err in our musicianship, more often than any other, would be in the extremes of loudness and faster tempos. Fortissimo climaxes become distorted from the blend standpoint because voices are asked to produce a sound far too loud for their inherent strength. They spread in focus and may produce a wobble at the end of the climax simply because the muscular strength of the body and vocal mechanism cannot meet the demands of the conductor.

A passage marked *allegro* may be taken at such a speed that the words become garbled. A continuing sequence of eighth notes will become faster and faster if the conductor does not lay back on the tempo and ask the singers to "overenunciate." Overenunciation is the only cure for an acceleration of a sequence of fast-occurring eighth or sixteenth notes.

So, the composer must use a term to warn us, such as *allegro non troppo* (fast but not too much) or *forte non troppo* (loud but not too much).

In life, a key word to use as a guide would be *moderation*. The Bible tells us that we should be moderate in all things. We should follow moderation in each area of life. The care of our bodies, the work schedules we tackle, our resources. We may appropriate the wisdom and guidance that the Lord gives to those who ask him in full measure.

There is only one aspect in the Christian's life where *troppo* does not apply—that is in our total commitment to Jesus Christ. It is impossible to be too committed to the One who said,

> I have loved you with an everlasting love; therefore with loving-kindness I have drawn you.

Jeremiah 31:3

Tutti

(tŏŏt′tē)

All together. The entire ensemble.

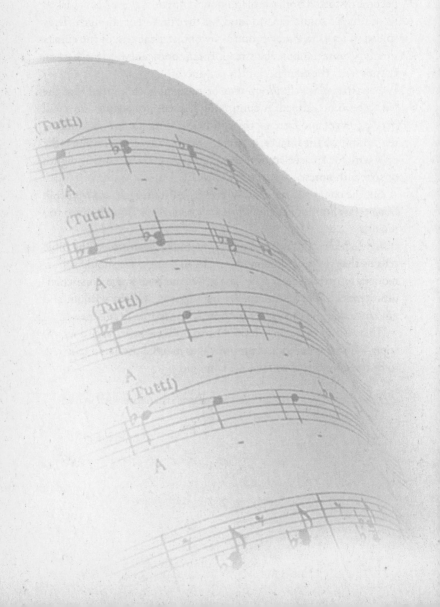

*I*n a choral or instrumental arrangement, there are times when individual sections will carry the theme or main line of the melody exclusively. The balance of the musicians will remain *tacet* until called upon by the conductor as indicated in his master score.

The term that will call the remaining voices and instruments into action is *tutti*. These same voices and instruments will join the entire ensemble, and once again the basic harmonic structure will become evident to the listener.

There is a certain strength that each musician will gain from the knowledge that everyone is functioning together and in harmony. The results will hopefully meet the standards that the composer indicated in his original score.

The call for a complete function of the body of Christ as a total unit or cohesive ensemble is already indicated to us in God's Word. We are to work together as believers, loving one another and fulfilling the law of God.

In a time when society is rampant with violence, theft, divisions, and despair, Christians must work together as an ensemble directed by Jesus Christ. How important it is to work cooperatively in such a way that our music will praise God, strengthen the believer, and extend salvation to the unsaved. Then will come the joy and fulfillment of following the Master Score together.

> But God, who is rich in mercy, because of His great love with which He loved us, even when we were dead in trespasses made us alive together with Christ . . . and raised us up together, and made us sit together in the heavenly places in Christ Jesus, that in the ages to come He might show the exceeding riches of His grace in His kindness toward us in Christ Jesus.
>
> Ephesians 2:4–7

Vivace

(vē vah'chěh)

Lively, brisk, animated.

*D*r. Theodore Baker indicates that *vivace* as a tempo mark standing by itself calls for a movement equaling or exceeding *allegro* (quick—literally cheerful). If it were to exceed *allegro*, it would go to *presto* (very fast) or *prestissimo* (as fast as possible).

Nevertheless, a tempo marked *vivace* indicates a very fast speed but a speed characterized by a controlled vitality. In a musical organization this is the responsibility of the director, for they must not lead their musicians at such a rate that, through technical insufficiencies, the fabric of the piece would become acoustically blurred or disintegrate into unintelligibility. It must remain animated with cohesion and clarity.

The power of the presence of the Spirit of Christ within the heart of the Christian musician is life giving and energy fulfilling. As the tempo *vivace* will bring to music a quality of liveliness, so Jesus Christ brings life abundantly with all its dimension of majesty, sovereignty, dominion, and power.

In Christ is the fulfillment of the greatest potential for every musician. In Christ is the reality of a "new song."

> He has put a new song in my mouth—Praise unto our God; many will see it and fear, and will trust in the Lord.
>
> Psalm 40:3

May this new song of salvation and redemption reflect an integrity and an excellence worthy of the Lord, and may it be evidence of the controlled vitality of a new life.

A Word to Directors
and Ministers of Music

*I*n my years as a director in the field of Christian church music, I have learned that our role of spiritual and musical leadership is heavy with responsibility. On the one hand, it can produce the greatest experiences of achievement and joy of any profession. On the other hand it can lead one along a path of misunderstanding, frustration, and bitterness if the Lord is not leading, guiding, and protecting in the total situation. Only a prayerful, obedient walk of faith in relation to the Lord Jesus Christ will bring encouragement, satisfaction, and a valid spiritual victory.

There are four areas in which the head of the music department must operate and relate to, with a highly developed sensitivity: the area of the ministerial staff, the area of the singers and instrumentalists, the area of the general congregation, and the area of the young people. None of these situations will be easy. However, with prayerful spiritual integrity, musical excellence, and the help of the Lord, we can build relationships based upon love and caring and a musical program of worship, edification, and evangelism.

Ego-serving attitudes must be cast aside. Standards, both spiritual and musical, must be established in order that the Lord might be continually glorified. Through his guiding presence and blessing, our music shall become worthy of his name, and the crescendos and diminuendos of our lives will be characterized by a beauty and strength beyond our fondest hopes and desires.

> And now, I entrust you to God and his care and to his wonderful words which are able to build your faith and give you all the inheritance of those who are set apart for himself.

Acts 20:32 TLB

Jack Coleman (1920–1985) was a graduate of USC with a bachelor's degree in music and a master's in education. He was the educational director for the Walt Disney Music Company and taught on all levels from elementary school to college. He served as music supervisor for Santa Ana Unified School District as well as coordinator of music for the Orange County Superintendent of Schools in Southern California. Coleman has many works of composition to his credit and was the director of music for First Baptist Church of Van Nuys, California, and for Grace Community Church in Panorama City, California.